THE PARENTING BOOK

11 Solutions to remedy the perils of

"Parenting as Usual"

OVIDILIO D. VÁSQUEZ

OVIDILIO D. VÁSQUEZ

ISBN-10: 1500109452
ISBN-13: 978-1500109455

About the Author

Ovidilio D. Vásquez is a *leading authority on motivation.* He enjoys delivering motivational speeches for parents and youth. He is also the founder of Speak Performance International. Ovidilio came to the United States in 2006 from the sugar cane fields of Aldea (village) El Chontel of La Gomera Escuintla Guatemala. He started to learn English in 2008 at a suburban high school. Even though his mom left him all alone in 2009 due to an emergency, Ovidilio D. Vásquez worked swing shifts in warehouses to support himself through high school and was able to graduate in 2011.

Once he graduated, Ovidilio received Business Management classes from Chabot College. In 2013 he founded Speak Performance International and is now traveling across the United States motivating parents and youth, teaching parents "How to Raise Positive Kids in a Negative World" and teaching youth "How to Overcome Adversity." He is also the creator of "Author In 90 Days" System.

Dedication

This book is especially dedicated to five of the most important people in my life. The order of their names does not matter. I love them with all my heart. They have supported me in my upbringing since I can remember. The person I am today is not self-made; I am very happy to say that I have these incredible people in my life who have helped me grow wiser and stronger.

To my mom, Verónica Aviles Sarceño, an incredible woman who has risked her life several times to be able to provide my brother and sister and me a better future. I love you, Mom. Thank you for all your hard work and dedication to my life.

To my girlfriend, Anali A. Muñoz, one of the most loving, patient, and supportive people I have ever met. She has been helping me push forward for the last five years of our relationship. Anali is one of the smartest people also. I have learned so much from her. Thank you for all you are doing for our relationship.

To my uncle, Juan Carlos Cruz, one of the wisest—if not the wisest—man in my family. My uncle Juan and Ana Ortiz have been there for me during tough times. Without the help, love, and support from my uncle Juan and Ana, I would not be where I am today.

He has been a crucial part of my journey. Thank you for all your advice. I love you very much, Uncle Juan. Thank you for always believing in me.

To my aunt, Gabriela Cruz Sarceño, one of the hardest working women I have ever seen. Thank you for being there in my high school times when I needed help the most. You are definitely part of my education foundation success. Thank you for believing in me and encouraging me to continue to grow as a person. Thank you for showing me by example to have high standards when it comes to having a work ethic. Thank you for gifting me my graduation ring with my uncle Juan. I love you and you will always be close to my heart.

To Dr. Thomas, by far the best English teacher I came across when I barely knew how to say, "How are you?" I met Dr. Thomas in a summer class in my high school. He had a unique approach to making all his students talk in class. But not just talking.

We were speaking in "English" and I quote English because we were in an English Language Learner class. So, we did what we could to learn and practice it. There was a very shy student. She would never talk. She was an introvert but when Dr. Thomas came into the room and started teaching, even she would speak. That is how good Dr. Thomas is.

Thank you for being very friendly and engaging when teaching. I very much appreciate your assistance with my first book. You will always be part of my success story.

Contents

Foreword

I met Ovidilio Vasquez in a summer English as a second language class at Tennyson High School in Hayward, California. I was teaching ESL levels 3-5 in one class with three different textbooks representing the three different levels. Ovidilio had been in the country less than a year, yet he was in level three. This was remarkable because it usually takes students five years to progress through the different levels. On average, second language learners take five years to attain fluency in a foreign language. Why was Ovidilio moving so quickly? Why was he a leader in the class even though he was in the lowest level in that group? Why was he able to progress out of level three into level four with only a two-month (instead of a year) class?

In short, Ovidilio is a remarkable person! It doesn't surprise me that he is writing his first book at such a young age—twenty-three years young. He owes his success to three character traits—hard work, charisma, and happiness. He always works hard and does his best for the right reasons. He is not motivated by grades or external rewards; he simply wants to improve. He is very charismatic.

As a junior in high school who spoke very little English, he rose to leadership roles without trying—people simply wanted to get to know him better. Finally, everyone likes to be around happy people. They are inspiring and fun. I am fortunate to have had the experience of teaching him, yet, even better, watching him grow and develop into a strong young man.

This book and Ovidilio's motivational speeches are designed to help parents instill the best character traits in their children by addressing some essential positive parenting techniques. Ovidilio's insights come from his own personal path to enlightenment as well as his observations of his peers.

His youth could easily have been a detriment to his chosen career path—that of a motivational speaker. Instead it provides a unique perspective on young people that needs to be heard by parents and young people alike. Enjoy his book and, if possible, get him to speak to your local group of parents and/or young adults. It will be a part of your own personal growth.

Paul M. Thomas, Ed.D.

Acknowledgements

There are many people I would love to thank for being a part of my life and who have supported me through my journey to becoming the most successful story of my family. You were all an inspiration for this book to come out to the world.

Mi familia: Francisco Chinchilla, Rubila Gabriela, (R.I.P. Edilson Chinchilla), Nery, Glen Sagastume, Manuel Sagastume, Yoni Mauricio Sánchez, and Zoila Mariela Ramírez.

My friends: Justin Méndez, Tashina Combs, Randie Ellington, Sabir Lomidze, Luis Hernández, Vianey Hernández, José Mendoza, Marina Mendoza, Giovanny Velásquez, Mike Alexander, Julio Palencia, Miguelina Palencia, Humberto Corado, special gratitude to Quetzalcoatl Garces y Liss Aguilar.

My former teachers now good friends: Paul M. Thomas, Ed.D., Miroslaba Velo Egonmwan, Donna De Leon, Diana Vazquez, Susan Reneberg, Melissa Morriss, Amy Kohl, special gratitude to Elsa Zamora, and "Mama" Diana Levy.

My virtual mentors, the ones responsible for my personal growth: Tony Robbins, Jim Rohn, Zig Ziglar, Les Brown, Victor Antonio, Brian Tracy, Earl Shoaff, John C. Maxwell, Dale Carnegie, Dr. Norman Vincent Peale, Kevin Trudeau, Joel Osteen, Napoleon Hill, Cesar Lozano, Alex Dey, Ruben Mata, James Malinchak, Dr. Matt James, Albert Einstein, Nikola Tesla, T. Harv Eker, Robert Kiyosaki, Arnold Schwarzenegger, Charles Tremendous Jones, Og Mandino, W. Clement Stone, Dr. Wayne Dyer, Andrew Carnegie, Dr. Stephen R. Covey, George S. Clason, Lao Tzu, Warren Buffett, Bill Gates, Steve Jobs, and many more…

In case I missed anyone, all of you have a very special place in my heart!

Let's begin with poetry that will hopefully inspire you to go on and read this quick but powerful book. Enjoy!

BY: Diana Loomans

If I had my child to raise over again,
I'd finger paint more, and point the finger less.
I'd do less correcting, and more connecting.
I'd take my eyes off my watch, and watch with my eyes.
I would care to know less, and know to care more.
I'd take more hikes and fly more kites.
I'd stop playing serious, and seriously play.
I'd run through more fields, and gaze at more stars.
I'd do more hugging, and less tugging.
I would be firm less often, and affirm much more.
I'd build self-esteem first, and the house later.
I'd teach less about the love of power,
And more about the power of love.
It matters not whether my child is big or small,
from this day forth, I'll cherish it all.

BY: Diana Loomans

From: *100 Ways to Build Self-Esteem and Teach Values*

Please visit her at: *www.dianaloomans.com*

Why Kids place parents in homecare.

By: Dr. Charles Larry Psychologist

You didn't feed me, you took me to McDonalds.

You didn't play with me, you bought me a bicycle.

You didn't study with me, you bought me a computer.

You didn't take care of me, you sent me to daycare.

You didn't entertain me, you bought me a DVD.

Why should I take care of you? I don't even know you.

By: Dr. Charles Larry Psychologist

Besides sharing with you those two beautiful poems, I want to also help you realize that kids do not see the world the way we do. How? You might ask. Allow me to illustrate it with a story.

Seven Wonders of the World

A group of students were asked to list what they thought were the present Seven Wonders of the World. Though there were some disagreements, the following received the most votes:

1. *Egypt's Great Pyramids*

2. *Taj Mahal*

3. *Grand Canyon*

4. *Panama Canal*

5. *Empire State Building*

6. *St. Peter's Basilica*

7. *China's Great Wall*

While gathering the votes, the teacher noted that one student had not finished her paper yet. So she asked the girl if she was having trouble with her list. The girl replied, "Yes, a little. I couldn't quite make up my mind because there were so many."

The teacher said, "Well, tell us what you have, and maybe we can help." The girl hesitated, then read, "I think the Seven Wonders of the World are:

1. *to see*
2. *to hear*
3. *to touch*
4. *to taste*
5. *to feel*
6. *to laugh*
7. *to love*

The room was so quiet you could have heard a pin drop. The things we overlook as simple and ordinary and that we take for granted are truly wondrous!!

If wealth is the secret to happiness, then the rich should be dancing in the streets. But only poor kids do that.

If power ensures security, then top officials should walk unguarded. But people who live on a roadside feel more secure.

If beauty brings ideal relationships, then celebrities should have the best marriages. But they frequently have the worst relationships. That is why you should… Live simply…Walk humbly… Love genuinely!!!

Pers☻nal Devel☻pment

The question for this chapter is:
How can I become a successful person?

The key answer to this question is: You must educate yourself first in order to educate others. By reading this book you are enhancing your skills of how to deal with kids. You will improve the quality of your relationship with your kids by applying what I will share with you in this quick but powerful book. Enjoy!

First let me identify "success" in the words of the great Earl Nightingale: *"Success is the progressive realization of a worthy ideal."* Nightingale was the world's renowned self-development guru and author of *The Strangest Secret in the World, Lead the Field*, and countless invaluable productions that have changed millions of lives including mine.

Once you know what it is you are looking for, you will find it easier. When you want to travel to X city, most people use Google Maps, but unless you identify where you are traveling from it will not tell you how to get to point B.

To be more successful I also have been applying advice from Mr. Warren Buffett

Warren Buffett
On Earnings
Never depend on a single income. Make investment to create a second source.
On Spending
If you buy things you do not need, soon you will have to sell things you need.

On Savings

Do not save what is left after spending, but spend what is left after saving.

On Taking Risks

Never test the depth of a river with both feet.

On Investment

Do not put all eggs in one basket

On Expectation

Honesty is a very expensive gift. Do not expect it from cheap people.

"Whether you think you can, or you think you can't—you're right."
~ Henry Ford

When it comes to success, Zig Ziglar, the World's Greatest Motivator, advised us to think of the most successful person we know. It could be a man, could be a woman, could be your parents, could be your son, could be your daughter, could be a cousin, could be a neighbor, could be a preacher, could be a sales person, could be a teacher, could be a politician, could be a singer, or could be a writer—you get the idea.

Think of the most successful person you know; this person has to be someone who, if you cannot be you, you would say, "I want to be her" or "I want to be him." Do not include a rich person just because he or she is rich. Many people are rich in money and wealth but very poor in love. Now, think about the qualities that make that person successful.

Some qualities could be: somebody with a good positive mental attitude, someone with great faith, someone who has a desire to achieve more, someone with enthusiasm, somebody who is a good listener, somebody with a good sense of humor, somebody who has integrity, somebody who is consistent, somebody who has love in their life, somebody who is sincere, somebody who is an encourager, somebody who is a hard worker, and the list continues.

Now, think about this, are you a person who practices these qualities on a daily basis? Are you working on acquiring or improving these qualities? When you apply some effort in your daily routine to become someone with these qualities, a compound effect begins to take effect.

Think about this—if a person eats a burger with a big soda on a daily basis, does that person become BIG in the first two weeks of eating the same portion every day?

Probably not, but since he or she does it daily, the compound effect eventually kicks in and the person starts getting BIG. Once they are in that stage more problems begin to occur. As my good friend Justin Mendez, keynote speaker, would say in his "Mental Breakfast" speech, *"As days add up to weeks, weeks add up to months, and months add up to years… We reap the bountiful harvest of our habits."*

What habits are you implementing to get you towards being a more successful person? The person whom you choose as a role model, what habits do they have?

Are you ready to learn from them?   Are you ready to say goodbye to some of your habits and say hello to better ones?

"You have made some mistakes and you may not be where you want to be…but that has nothing to do with your future."
~ Zig Ziglar

Napoleon Hill in his book *Think and Grow Rich* mentioned the importance of a mission statement. Every successful person carries one with them. That serves as a focus point. I have included my mission statement that I developed when I made a firm decision to become what I desired.

Feel free to copy my mission statement and edit it so it fits your own situation.

"Goal: To Get Paid To Speak by July 1st 2013

I'm willing to read every day all the material that's needed to deliver a speech according to the requested topic. I'm willing to give up Family Guy and, instead, grow and expand my mind in positive terms so I can be able to be, do, and have more of that which I desire.

I'm willing to discipline myself in various situations so that I can make the choices I have to make instead of choices I want to make. I'm open to all possibilities and willing to go through all the procedures and obstacles that might come along. I'm willing to consciously think and act positive towards all situations in life, for I know and trust that everything that's happening and will happen is for my own good.

I'm willing to share 10% of my time and income so I can make an impact in my greater community. I'm committed to stay consistent and work hard in a smart way to see all these goals through and finally achieve my desired outcome. I trust and know that I have what it takes; therefore my goal is closer that I can currently imagine.

My purpose is to express my Willingness to Accept change, willingness to work hard and willingness to go the extra mile by being committed to do things differently, by being consistent with labor and by going beyond my goals to free up one extra day a week for family/personal time, become a Motivational Speaker, have more happiness and joy in life and obtain at least $100,000.00 by 12/19/2013."

I did not reach my goal of getting the $100k but I did reach my goal of being a paid speaker in 2013. When you are working towards your personal goal it is not going to be easy.

Easy is not always on the menu. It is hard but it is worth it. Be patient, be smart, be persistent, be a good apprentice, and, above all, keep the faith. Remember what Winston Churchill said, ***"Never, ever, ever, ever, ever, give up."***

Share this on Facebook and Twitter: #OVinspires
@OVinspires
*"It is better to be prepared for an opportunity and not
have one than to have an opportunity and not be
prepared."*
~Whitney M. Young, Jr.

I will also tell you this on the parenting side of
success. Do not aim for perfection. Nobody is
perfect; do not torture yourself with an
impossibly high bar for parenting success.
According to a study published in 2011 in the
journal *Personality and Individual Differences*, new
parents who believe society expects perfection
from them are more stressed and less confident
in their parenting skills.

And no wonder! Make an effort to ignore the
pressure, and you may find yourself a more
relaxed parent. Remember; slow and steady.
Enjoy every moment of it. Life is made up of
memorable moments. Prepare yourself every day.

Record your important thoughts and ideas on how to improve on your **Personal Development**

_____

_____

_____

_____

_____

_____

_____

_____

_____

_____

_____

_____

_____

_____

_____

_____

_____

_____

_____

_____

_____

_____

_____

_____

_____

_____

_____

Record your important thoughts and ideas on how to improve on your **Pers☺nal Devel☺pment**

_____

_____

_____

_____

_____

_____

_____

_____

_____

_____

_____

_____

_____

_____

_____

_____

_____

_____

_____

_____

_____

_____

_____

_____

_____

_____

_____

Record your important thoughts and ideas on how to improve on your **Personal Development**

_____
_____
_____
_____
_____
_____
_____
_____
_____
_____
_____
_____
_____
_____
_____
_____
_____
_____
_____
_____
_____
_____
_____

C☻mmunicati☻n

The question for this chapter is:
How do I build stronger communication with my kid?

The main reason teens do not talk much is because of puberty. It is not your fault, but it is your responsibility to break through and get to the heart of your teen. Here is what teens translate LOVE into, teens translate LOVE into TIME. They need your time! Be with your teen when they have difficulties communicating their feelings. Giving them your time is pretty much all you can do for them at that very moment.

Most middle school students cannot articulate their feelings. And sometimes they just do not understand what is going on inside of them. Most middle school students don't really understand what is going on in their surroundings and they do not need you to tell them to return to their old selves when they were little. They just need your time. Avoid lecturing or nagging. If a conversation goes on for too long, it is going to be perceived as a lecture.

Sit down and make a list of questions that you genuinely want to know the answer to. Here are some examples:

Who is your best friend?
What makes him/her your best friend?
Who is somebody in your school you have a hard time getting along with?
Why do you think that happens?
Who is your favorite teacher?
Why is he/she your favorite teacher?
Who is your worst teacher?
Why is he/she your worst teacher?
What are you looking forward to?
Where would you like to go on vacation as a family?
What would we do?
What is your favorite song?

Now ask them to play it for you. Ask why that song means so much to them. The goal of this is for you to get in their mind and understand what is going on. Practice not talking, ask the question and listen actively.

Being a parent is being a student of your kid. Be with them. They need time with you. Even if they do not say it, your kid needs you to be with him or her. Here is a valuable piece of information I found while reading on **www.LiveScience.com**. Visit their website, they have a lot of worthwhile information.

"LOL Joking Helps"

"Lighten up! Joking with your kids helps set them up for social success, according to research presented at the Economic and Social Research Councils' Festival of Social Science 2011. When parents joke and pretend, it gives young kids the tools to think creatively, make friends and manage stress. So feel free to play court jester, your kids will thank you later."

For more information please visit them at: **www.LiveScience.com**

Record your important thoughts and ideas on how to improve on your **Communication** Perhaps add a list of questions to ask your kid.

_____
_____
_____
_____
_____
_____
_____
_____
_____
_____
_____
_____
_____
_____
_____
_____
_____
_____
_____
_____
_____
_____
_____

Record your important thoughts and ideas on
how to improve on your **C☺mmunicati☺n**
Perhaps add a list of questions to ask your kid.

_____

_____

_____

_____

_____

_____

_____

_____

_____

_____

_____

_____

_____

_____

_____

_____

_____

_____

_____

_____

_____

_____

_____

Record your important thoughts and ideas on how to improve on your **C☺mmunicati☺n** Perhaps add a list of questions to ask your kid.

_____
_____
_____
_____
_____
_____
_____
_____
_____
_____
_____
_____
_____
_____
_____
_____
_____
_____
_____
_____
_____
_____
_____
_____
_____
_____

Depression

The question for this chapter is:
What if my kid is depressed?

"Be helpful when you see a person without a smile give them yours."
~ Zig Ziglar

Even if you remember the practical content from this quick but powerful book, I want you to remember the stories that come with it. Tales that will help you get your point across. I want to make it as simple as possible for you to have a successful relationship with your kids.

Here is a tale to assist you when you're talking to your kids or other kids about depression.

A Battle of Two Wolves Inside Us All

An old Cherokee told his grandson, "My son, there's a battle between two wolves inside us all. One is Evil. It's anger, jealousy, greed, resentment, inferiority, lies and ego. The other is Good. It's joy, peace, love, hope, humility, kindness and truth." The boy thought about it and asked, "Grandfather, which wolf wins?"

The old man quietly replied, "The one you feed.

That beautiful tale says a lot. Use it and explain to your kid that they get to choose which wolf wins the battle between feeling DOWN or feeling ENERGIZED and full of joy. Be sure to contribute to that joy for them to feel cared for. Remember to remind him or her to FEED THE GOOD WOLF.

You need to understand that depression is an incredibly big issue. It may be easy to diagnose by its outward symptoms, but the root causes of depression are not so simple. There are multiple reasons why a teen might be going through depression. Here is what you can do.

First: It could be chemical; your teen has double the amount of hormones raging through his/her body right now. It is very possible that their brain does not make enough of a certain chemical, just as diabetics do not produce enough insulin for the body. Your teen might be in a situation where there is a chemical reason for the depression.

Second: Depression can be caused by social issues as well. Think about going through junior high and high school. It is a time in your life filled with tons of social situations that are stressful, dramatic and really difficult to navigate, particularly when you are a fourteen, fifteen, or seventeen. A really bad day can seem really like the end of your world. Your teen could be depressed because of perceived rejection by peers or some sort of difficult social circumstance they run into in junior high and/or high school.

Third: Depression can be emotional: Your teen's emotions tend to run out of control. Because this is no fault of their own they lack the ability to put life into proper prospective.

They are sort of dealing with these grown up issues, but they have only had 15 years on this planet so they lack that perspective that maybe you or I would have. Things seem like the end of the world, when really they are not.

Do you remember that thing that happened to you when you were a kid and you just thought your entire world was crashing down and everyone was laughing at you, mocking you, knew about things, and this and that, when really some days went by and people had moved on to something else?

Fourth: It could be a moral issue. Depression can be caused by moral issues, meaning if your teen is secretly doing something he or she knows is wrong, they will inevitably feel guilt for it. You know, we all have a conscience. Violating it causes a sense of disintegration. *I am not the person that I want to be but I am doing this thing that does not line up with who I want to be.*

This dichotomy can lead depression. That sort of disintegration of who I claim I want to be and who I think I could be with the choices that I am making and the kind of person who makes these bad choices.

Those are some of the reasons, but, ultimately, the point is this—the reasons for depression are various. It could be any one of those things. It could be a combination of two or more of those things. It could be something I did not even mention.

It is important to understand this is a new and complex issue. You, the parent, are going to have to do the hard work in figuring out exactly what is at the bottom of this. I wish I could give you an easy formula. The fact of the matter is your kid is a complex person just like we all are.

In many cases the loving, unconditional support of the parent or a caring adult who listens, who does not judge, who cares, and who offers council where appropriate is sometimes enough.

Sometimes that is not enough. Sometimes there are situations where more is required. And, if you find yourself in a situation where your teen is descending into depression and it lasts for extended periods of time, it is time for you to seek professional help.

There is no shame in seeking professional help. Please do not let that shame or guilt of what will other people think and all of that get into your head. Most people on the planet should get counseled. As a parent, the good news is there is no professional training needed to care, to listen, to be there for them, and to be on their side.

As Brian Tracy, international business motivational speaker would advise: Be the main source of unconditional love for your teen. Always love them unconditionally 100%. If anyone asks them how much you love them, their answer should be, "My parent loves me 100%." But that will not be their answer if you do not let them know and show it.

Share this on Facebook and Twitter: #OVinspires @OVinspires

Be the main source of unconditional love for your kids. Always love them unconditionally 100%

Record your important thoughts and ideas on
how to help your kid with **Depression**

_____

_____

_____

_____

_____

_____

_____

_____

_____

_____

_____

_____

_____

_____

_____

_____

_____

_____

_____

_____

_____

_____

_____

_____

_____

_____

_____

Record your important thoughts and ideas on how to help your kid with **Depression**

_____

_____

_____

_____

_____

_____

_____

_____

_____

_____

_____

_____

_____

_____

_____

_____

_____

_____

_____

_____

_____

_____

_____

_____

Record your important thoughts and ideas on how to help your kid with **Depression**

_____

_____

_____

_____

_____

_____

_____

_____

_____

_____

_____

_____

_____

_____

_____

_____

_____

_____

_____

_____

_____

_____

_____

_____

_____

_____

_____

SEX

The question for this chapter is:
How do I talk to my kid about sex?

As humans we are very curious creatures. If
you are religious you can use the Bible and let
your teen know that the Bible says that premarital
sex or sex outside of marriage is wrong. You can
let your son know that if he and his girlfriend get
involved in sex, he will never get to know the girl.
That might sound strange but once sex is
involved, that is all the boy and the girl think
about.

They will try like you cannot believe to do it
every time they can wherever they can. Tell your
teen that if he or she gets involved in sex, they
will never talk about children, careers, values,
where they are going to live. All those things
make an important contribution to a successful,
happy family.

Not only that, tell them that they will become
liars. Your teen will lie to you, will hide from you,
will tell you he or she is going one place when in
reality they are going to another and the precious
relationship he has with you will be damaged.

Let your daughter know that if she gets pregnant, and let your son know that if his girlfriend gets pregnant, if you believe that abortion is not an option, they will have a baby. They will have to get married. They will probably have to give up college. They will have to give up their childhood.

It is going to be a very serious situation. Let them know that if they can control themselves now when they are at their height of sexual excitement, it will prepare them beautifully for marriage.

One of the beautiful things about it is if they refrain and the relationship breaks up, she will always be able to say, "My first serious boyfriend was <u>NAME</u> and he treated me like a lady and I am so grateful for that. If they get involved in sex, she will always say, "That little malefactor, look what he did to me." Remember she has to make the decision. He has to make the decision. It can make all the difference in the world when you teach your kid early on.

These are some of the things you can say to prevent strategies taking place in your kids' lives. Teach them what to say, how to refrain, teach them not to put themselves in compromising positions. If dope is being smoked do not even go in, if alcohol is being served, do not even go in.

How early can I talk to my child about sex?

In his program "The New Raising Positive Kids in a Negative World" Zig Ziglar recommends that you should begin talking to your children about sex as early as four years old. Sexual education must be taught by the parents if your beliefs about sexual activity are different than those of the teacher at school.

It is more likely that the teacher will teach his or her beliefs, not yours. Then you will be unhappy about what is going on in your kid's mind.

Many parents say, "I am going to wait until he or she asks." Do you really believe that your kid will ask you? Your kid probably will not even dare to bring up the subject. Let me share a story with you.

A father comes to his son and says, "Son, come here, I want to talk with you about sex." Kid replies, "Yes, Dad, what is it that you want to know?"

Keep this in mind. If you do not teach them at home, someone else will, and then it will probably be too late.

When you do any activities where the child is looking at you, it should be something the child can also participate in. You should start by teaching moral values and responsibilities. Many parents allow TV, radio, or internet to be their child's teacher. You must recognize that those are often sources of gossip and misrepresentation for the kids' minds.

Teach your kid about privacy. Always knock on their door when you are going in their room. That will teach them to always knock on yours when he or she wants to come in. When teaching your young child about sex, you can say, "Sex is something that parents, husbands and wives enjoy." When they are older, talk to them about it in greater detail.

If they are between ten and twelve years old, get them a book about sex. When your kid begins to read it, you always close every conversation with your child by saying, "Anytime you want to talk more about this just let me know, we will be more than happy to discuss it with you." You don't over educate them initially but you let it be crystal clear in the way you deal with the subject.

The father should talk to the son. The mother should talk to the daughter. Remember, a father can teach more to a daughter about guys in an hour than mother can teach them in months. Also, remember that a mother can teach more to a son about girls in an hour than a father can teach them about them in months. Do not ever tell them that sex is dirty. You cannot tell them their entire life that sex is dirty and then on their wedding night tell them that it is a gift from God or The Source.

Remind your teen that by not getting involved in sex, they do not have to worry about pregnancy. They do not have to worry about venereal disease. They do not have to worry about getting caught.

They do not have to worry about embarrassment. They do not have to worry about hiding things from you.

Dan Zadra said, *"Worry is a misuse of the imagination."* And **Muhammad Ali** said, *"The man who has no imagination has no wings."* Your kid will actually concentrate on being a better student. When they can focus in school then they will be successful in their studies.

"The successful warrior is the average man, with laser-like focus."
~ Bruce Lee

Record your important thoughts and ideas on how to talk to your kid about **Sex**

_____

_____

_____

_____

_____

_____

_____

_____

_____

_____

_____

_____

_____

_____

_____

_____

_____

_____

_____

_____

_____

_____

_____

_____

_____

_____

_____

Record your important thoughts and ideas on how to talk to your kid about **Sex**

_____
_____
_____
_____
_____
_____
_____
_____
_____
_____
_____
_____
_____
_____
_____
_____
_____
_____
_____
_____
_____
_____
_____
_____
_____
_____
_____
_____
_____
_____

Record your important thoughts and ideas on
how to talk to your kid about **Sex**

_____

_____

_____

_____

_____

_____

_____

_____

_____

_____

_____

_____

_____

_____

_____

_____

_____

_____

_____

_____

_____

_____

_____

_____

_____

_____

_____

_____

The Power of Apologies

The question for this chapter is:
How can I have confidence when talking to my kids?

Let's start off with a story that will help you understand the power of anger management first and then let's get into The Power of Apologies.

"LOVE YOU, DAD."

While a man was polishing his new car, his 4-year-old son picked up a stone & scratched lines on the side of the car. In anger, the man took the child's hand & hit it many times, not realizing he was using a wrench.

At the hospital, the child lost all his fingers due to multiple fractures. When the child saw his father ... with a painful look in eyes, he asked, "Dad, when will my fingers grow back?"

The man was so hurt and speechless. He went back to his car and kicked it a lot of times... Devastated by his own actions, sitting in front of that car he looked at the scratches. The child had written "LOVE YOU, DAD" The next day that man committed suicide.

Anger and love have no limits, so let the river of life flow in limits so that this fresh water stream is never scattered.

Always remember that "Things are to be used and people are to be loved." But the problem in today's world is that "People are being used & Things are being loved."

Keep that story in mind just in case you ever get angry. First find out the main reason your kid is doing what he or she is doing. Let's continue our journey.

Here is what teen expert Josh Shipp has to say on this. In order for you, as a parent, to give advice to your teen, you need to do some self-check assessment. Apologize to your teen when you have made a mistake. If you have never apologized to your kids in your life, something is missing.

One of the roles of the family is to teach kids how to give and receive forgiveness. Forgiveness is a crucial life skill. There are ways to effectively apologize and there are ways not to effectively apologize.

You cannot apologize by saying something like, "I am sorry, you are so stupid," "I am sorry that you overreacted," or "This is not the most right I have ever been." Those are not genuine apologies.

Life is about relationships. By apologizing to your teen it causes them to respect you more. When you offer an apology, be genuine. In order to apologize you have to genuinely want things to get better with that other person. You need to check yourself. If you are not willing to apologize, you might have some pride issues.

Make sure the other person knows that you authentically value them and their feelings. Another thing, do not make excuses. Your teen is going to learn a lot from what you say but they are going to learn the most from what you do. As Zig Ziglar would say, "Your children more attention pays to what you do than what you say." Actions speak louder than words.

Here are phrases you should not use to apologize:

1. I didn't mean to: *Even though you did not mean to, you still hurt them.*

2. Just forget about it: *Take full responsibility for what you did. Your kid will learn that from you.*

3. Nobody is perfect: *Of course nobody is perfect. But if you do not show that you truly care why would you expect him or her to care later on?*

Before the apology even happens be ready to make things right. If you broke a promise, stop what you are doing now and value your word. Communicate how to plan on changing. The last thing you want to be is a parent who apologizes for the same thing over and over.

Communicate to your teen that you intend to stop and do it. Figure out what the next step is and go ahead. Let them know that you might mess up from time to time, and that is fine. Your kid knows that you are at least trying. They do not expect perfection from you. Do not try to control their response. Drop your expectation of how you want your teen to reply.

They might not accept your apology now but eventually they will recognize that you did it to the best of your ability and you were honest. The bottom line on apologies is how they take it is up to them.

Sometimes it takes more maturity to accept an apology than to deliver one. So, as a parent, model for your kid on how to responsibly and maturely deliver an apology, take responsibly, commit to changing, and hope that by modeling this behavior they will adopt it as their own.

Record your important thoughts and ideas on how to help your kid through **The Power of Apologies**

_____

_____

_____

_____

_____

_____

_____

_____

_____

_____

_____

_____

_____

_____

_____

_____

_____

_____

_____

_____

_____

_____

_____

_____

_____

Record your important thoughts and ideas on how to help your kid through **The Power ☺f Apol☺gies**

_____

_____

_____

_____

_____

_____

_____

_____

_____

_____

_____

_____

_____

_____

_____

_____

_____

_____

_____

_____

_____

_____

_____

_____

_____

Record your important thoughts and ideas on how to help your kid through **The Power of Apologies**

_____
_____
_____
_____
_____
_____
_____
_____
_____
_____
_____
_____
_____
_____
_____
_____
_____
_____
_____
_____
_____
_____
_____
_____
_____
_____

Verbal and/or Physical Abuse

The question for this chapter is:
How do I stop my kid from talking back?

Let's start off with this: there is absolutely no excuse for abuse ever, ever, and ever, period, end of story. If you are being verbally attacked by your kid, here is a strategy. As a parent, you may not realize how much control you have and actually how many privileges you control.

You provide your kid transportation, a cell phone, perhaps a computer, clothing, approval for going out to places, and rides to fun places. You have a lot more power than you sometimes think. You must begin to leverage that power. Here is what you can do:

First: Refuse to fight back. As Dr. Phill says, "You do not have to attend every dog fight you are invited to." Meaning just because your kid lashes out at you with verbal abuse, it does not mean you have to reciprocate with verbal abuse.

Do not yell back. It is really hard to yell at someone when they are not yelling back. It is hard to fight with someone when they are not fighting back with you.

When this happens, simply say this to them: "I love you too much to argue with you and I will be happy to talk with you about this when you are kind."

Once you say those words, you simply turn around and you walk away. You are the adult. You need to lead by example and show them what it looks like to diffuse a hostile situation.

Second: You need to provide real consequences. The only thing you have to legally provide for your kid is food, clothing, and a place to sleep. Everything else is a treat. Start stripping away the extras. The only place your kid has to be is doing school hours. So, start stripping away their free time including any extracurricular activities band, theater, and sports.

If they are being abusive, these sorts of things are privileges. I want to warn you never to trip away privileges with an evil grin. You never want to shout or scream with a posture of revenge.

You always discipline your kid with a broken heart. When a kid is being verbally abusive, you start taking away their privileges.

You could say something like, "I am happy to provide these great privileges to kids who treat me with respect. If you choose to be verbally abusive to me I will have no choice but to take away all these privileges that I have for you.

"I am more than willing to remove everything out of your room if that is what it takes, except for the mattress." You have to have the strength to take away their privileges.

If you do not do this, unfortunately, sadly, and unfairly, the abuse will continue. Train your kid how to treat you. If you fail to implement these consequences nothing will change. There is nothing you can do to change your kid's attitude.

The best way to get through to them is to have them experience the devastating consequences of their own actions. The goal of this discipline is for them to be angry with their own choice that they made, not angry at you. Remember, discipline is something you do for them, not to them.

Record your important thoughts and ideas on how to help your kid in case of **Verbal and/or Physical Abuse**

_____

_____

_____

_____

_____

_____

_____

_____

_____

_____

_____

_____

_____

_____

_____

_____

_____

_____

_____

_____

_____

_____

_____

_____

_____

_____

_____

_____

Record your important thoughts and ideas on how to help your kid in case of **Verbal and/or Physical Abuse**

_____

_____

_____

_____

_____

_____

_____

_____

_____

_____

_____

_____

_____

_____

_____

_____

_____

_____

_____

_____

_____

_____

_____

_____

_____

Record your important thoughts and ideas on how to help your kid in case of **Verbal and/or Physical Abuse**

_____

_____

_____

_____

_____

_____

_____

_____

_____

_____

_____

_____

_____

_____

_____

_____

_____

_____

_____

_____

_____

_____

_____

_____

Drugs

The question for this chapter is:
How do I help my kid deal with drugs?

The behavior and patterns associated with alcohol and drug abuse can vary. Here is how addiction to drugs and alcohol works: Teens start using drugs out of curiosity and typically have fun. Then kids continue drug use to stop feeling bad. Drugs and alcohol warp dopamine production. Dopamine is simply the happiness chemical in your brain that makes you feel good.

When your teen uses drugs or alcohol their dopamine levels get drastically altered. In many cases the only way they can get dopamine is through drugs and alcohol use. Some teenagers are using drugs simply to feel normal. This is all about brain chemistry; the kid needs the drug just to get to a level of normalcy. This is how drug addiction works neurologically.

As a parent here is what you need to do; if your teen is addicted to drugs or alcohol things obviously must change. You need to change the natural parenting role with a teen that is addicted.

You should no longer see yourself as a caregiver but rather as a landlord. A mom or a dad has instincts to care for their teen such as wash their clothes, clean their room, give them money, and these sorts of things.

A teen who is a potential drug addict would actually take advantage of this parental instinct and use this 'weakness' to get what they want— more money out of you, bailed out of trouble, and such like.

See yourself as a landlord not as a caregiver. This prevents you from enabling your teen to continue their addiction. The landlord approach keeps things more manageable. This is going to include: clear, written boundaries with non-emotional consequences that are executed in a matter of fact way. Think about it. If a landlord has a tenant who has broken an agreement the landlord simply executes a plan of action to demand change.

Here is what you should do. Simply write a contract like a landlord. Make sure this contract is written in advance non-emotionally. This should be done when you are feeling cool. Keep in mind nothing will work unless there are clear consequences. You need to have consequences that are fair, clear, predetermined, and delivered with compassion.

It might seem heartless to see yourself as a landlord, but it is not. It is tough and it is fair and, most importantly, is effective in keeping parents away from enabling. It positions you to truly help your teen understand the consequences of drug or alcohol use while getting the help they desperately need to get sober and clean.

This is the bottom line. You are helping your teen to be clean and sober as well as to be equipped with healthy decision-making skills, so they can make the right decisions for themselves. This is dramatically important and critical because, sometimes, as parents, you enable and love your kid in a certain situation when what you should do is hand the problem back to them.

Your teen is making the decision to use drugs. Your teen has that problem, but you take it on yourself. Now you feel like you have the problem instead of your teen. Create a contract you are going to use and implement.

What it will do is hand the problem back to your teen. Your teen will feel the weight of the decision that he is making so he will be naturally motivated to change. This is his responsibility. You can help him with this, but this is ultimately your teen's life and therefore his responsibility.

Record your important thoughts and ideas on
how to help your kid in case of use of **Drugs**

_____

_____

_____

_____

_____

_____

_____

_____

_____

_____

_____

_____

_____

_____

_____

_____

_____

_____

_____

_____

_____

_____

_____

_____

_____

Record your important thoughts and ideas on how to help your kid in case of use of **Drugs**

_____
_____
_____
_____
_____
_____
_____
_____
_____
_____
_____
_____
_____
_____
_____
_____
_____
_____
_____
_____
_____
_____
_____
_____
_____

Record your important thoughts and ideas on how to help your kid in case of use of **Drugs**

_____

_____

_____

_____

_____

_____

_____

_____

_____

_____

_____

_____

_____

_____

_____

_____

_____

_____

_____

_____

_____

_____

_____

_____

_____

_____

_____

_____

Friendly Advice

The question for this chapter is:
How do I give more friendly advice?

"The solution of all adult problems tomorrow depends in large measure upon the way our children grow up today."
~ Margaret Mead, Anthropologist

Here is a friendly piece of advice you can give your kids:
Life is Like a Camera
FOCUS on what is important.
CAPTURE the good times.
DEVELOP from the negatives.
And if things do not work out… Just take another SHOT.

I will refer again to Zig Ziglar's teachings. He states that, in order for a parent to understand their children, a parent needs to get down to their kid's intellectual level, yet lead them. There is a difference between having your kid as a friend vs. having him or her as your child. The kid does not need another friend. They make them at school. Friends are generally about the same age.

The kid needs a parent who has mature judgment and who will make all decisions based on the best interests of the child, not what the kid wants but what he or she needs. You are not here to please your kids. You are here to guide, to direct, and to encourage them.

If your child doesn't want to obey when you tell him not to go out with his friends, explain that his friends might be his friend for days, weeks, and maybe months, but you will be his parent forever and you love him very much. As Brian Tracy would say, be the main source of love for your kids. Once they know that, they are more likely to obey your rules. Allow the kid to make the decision that is in his or her best interest.

I want to share with you this sequence of questions I came across while reading a parenting article on Lifehack.org When I read this article, YOU were in my mind—a caring parent like you who is looking for a few more strategies to better the relationships at home.

"The Secret to Raising Happy Kids"
by

ERIN KURT
Lifehack Expert since Nov, 2009

1. *Pretend you had a video camera following you around all day. What would that video look like?*

2. *Would it show you: Rushing around from one activity to another?*

3. *Barking commands?*

4. *Constantly talking or having noise around like the radio or TV?*

5. *Speaking quickly, in a hurried, worried, stressed or anxious tone?*

6. *Constantly providing or being the entertainment for your child?*

   OR

7. *Living life slowly?*

8. *Laughing and smiling a lot?*

9. *Enjoying moments of silence, not feeling the need to say anything or ask any questions?*

10. *Enjoying alone time, while your child enjoys their own?*

11. *Doing an activity with your child that you BOTH enjoy?*

Record your important thoughts and ideas on how to give **friendly advice to your kid**

_____
_____
_____
_____
_____
_____
_____
_____
_____
_____
_____
_____
_____
_____
_____
_____
_____
_____
_____
_____
_____
_____
_____
_____
_____
_____

Record your important thoughts and ideas on how to give **friendly advice to your kid**

_____
_____
_____
_____
_____
_____
_____
_____
_____
_____
_____
_____
_____
_____
_____
_____
_____
_____
_____
_____
_____
_____
_____
_____

Record your important thoughts and ideas on how to give **friendly advice to your kid**

_____

_____

_____

_____

_____

_____

_____

_____

_____

_____

_____

_____

_____

_____

_____

_____

_____

_____

_____

_____

_____

_____

_____

_____

Self-Esteem

The question for this chapter is:
How can I elevate my child's self-esteem?

Share this with your kids:

IF EGG IS BROKEN BY OUTSIDE FORCE LIFE ENDS. IF BROKEN BY INSIDE FORCE LIFE BEGINS. GREAT THINGS ALWAYS BEGIN FROM INSIDE

If an egg is broken by outside forces, life ends.
If an egg is broken by inside force, life begins.
Great things always happen from inside.

Your kids need to learn and be aware of the importance of their thoughts and feelings about themselves. You will now be able to provide support for them to grow their self-esteem to higher levels.

This will lead to better performance, better grades, better attitude, and better relationships outside and at home. Make sure to encourage them to *accept themselves*, to *value themselves*, to *forgive themselves*, to *bless themselves*, to *trust themselves*, to *love themselves*, and to *empower themselves*.

As I was reading through **www.kidshealth.org** I found this article very simple and easy to understand. Go ahead and check their website for additional stories to share with your child.

"You cannot touch it, but it affects how you feel. You cannot see it, but it might be there when you look at yourself in the mirror. You cannot hear it, but it is there when you talk about yourself or when you think about yourself. What is this important but mysterious thing? **It is your self-esteem!**

What Is Self-Esteem?

To understand self-esteem, it helps to break the term into two words. Let's first take a look at the word esteem (say: es-teem), which means that someone or something is important, special, or valuable.

For example, if you really admire your friend's dad because he volunteers at the fire department, it means you hold him in high esteem. And the special trophy for the most valuable player on a team is often called an esteemed trophy. This means the trophy stands for an important accomplishment.

And self means, well, you! So, put the two words together and it is easier to see what self-esteem is. It is how much you value yourself and how important you think you are. It is how you see yourself and how you feel about the things you can do.

Self-esteem is not about bragging; it is about getting to know what you are good at and not so good at. A lot of us think about how much we like other people or things, but do not really think much about whether we like ourselves.

It is not about thinking you are perfect, because nobody is perfect. Even if you think some other kids are good at everything, you can be sure they have things they are good at and things that are difficult for them.

Self-esteem means seeing yourself in a positive way that is realistic, which means that it is the truth. So if you know you are really good at piano but cannot draw so well, you can still have great self-esteem!

The first step is awareness, be aware of what you want. You now have a better understanding about what self-esteem is and, by increasing self-esteem in yourself, you will pass that positive energy along to your kids.

www.kidshealth.org

Share this on Facebook and Twitter: #OVinspires @OVinspires
Self-esteem is not about bragging. It is about getting to know what you are good at and not so good at.

I want to share with you a self-talk that I learned from some of my virtual mentors. The method of autosuggestion is the hypnotic or subconscious adoption of an idea that one has originated oneself, e.g. through repetition of verbal statements to oneself in order to change behavior.

This self-talk will help you and your kid increase self-esteem. Read it in the morning and afternoon every day. Read it in front of a mirror to make a greater impact. Remember, the eyes are the windows to the soul.

When reading these lines, touch your heart. Feelings are the most important factor to every human being.

1. *I deeply and completely love myself.*
2. *I believe in myself despite others' opinions.*
3. *I feel good about taking care of my own needs.*
4. *I am comfortable being myself around others.*
5. *I am a unique and valuable person just as I am.*
6. *I am becoming more and more confident.*
7. *I love myself just the way I am.*
8. *I like the way I handle challenges.*
9. *I feel good and good is attracted to me.*
10. *I openly express my needs and feelings.*
11. *I am my own unique self—special, creative and wonderful.*
12. *I love and accept myself.*
13. *I am healthy and happy.*
14. *I am inherently worthy as a person.*
15. *I accept and learn from my mistakes.*

*Sometimes the chains that
prevent us from being free
are more mental than physical.*

Record your important thoughts and ideas on
how to help your kid in case of
Low Self-Esteem

_____

_____

_____

_____

_____

_____

_____

_____

_____

_____

_____

_____

_____

_____

_____

_____

_____

_____

_____

_____

_____

_____

_____

_____

Record your important thoughts and ideas on
how to help your kid in case of
Low Self-Esteem

_____

_____

_____

_____

_____

_____

_____

_____

_____

_____

_____

_____

_____

_____

_____

_____

_____

_____

_____

_____

_____

_____

_____

_____

_____

_____

Record your important thoughts and ideas on how to help your kid in case of
Low Self-Esteem

_____

_____

_____

_____

_____

_____

_____

_____

_____

_____

_____

_____

_____

_____

_____

_____

_____

_____

_____

_____

_____

_____

_____

_____

Building Character

The question for this chapter is:
How do I build my kid's positive character?

"We may not be able to prepare the future for our children, but we can at least prepare our children for the future."

~ Franklin D. Roosevelt

Here are 3 rules to teach your kids so they can be a person of good character.

First*; teach them not to forget the person who helps them.*
Second*; teach them not to hate the person who loves them.*
Third*; teach them not to cheat the person who trusts them.*

Life is simple, you can teach your kids those three rules and you are on your way to raising a kid with great character.

You will also build your kid's character by teaching about compassion in the family. This will help you raise a positive kid in a negative world. Remember, your kids pay more attention to what you do than what you say.

Let me share with you a story I read in *www.MoralStories.org*

"Making Relationships Special"

When I was a kid, my mom liked to make breakfast food for dinner every now and then. And I remember one night in particular when she had made dinner after a long, hard day at work. On that evening so long ago, my mom placed a plate of eggs, sausage and extremely burned biscuits in front of my dad. I remember waiting to see if anyone noticed! Yet all dad did was reach for his biscuit, smile at my mom and ask me how my day was at school. I don't remember what I told him that night, but I do remember watching him smear butter and jelly on that biscuit and eat every bite!

When I got up from the table that evening, I remember hearing my mom apologize to my dad for burning the biscuits. And I'll never forget what he said: "Honey, I love burned biscuits."

Later that night, I went to kiss Daddy good night and I asked him if he really liked his biscuits burned. He wrapped me in his arms and said, "Your momma put in a hard day at work today and she's real tired. And besides—a little burned biscuit never hurt anyone!"

Moral: Life is full of imperfect things and imperfect people. I'm not the best at everything; I forget birthdays, and anniversaries just like everyone else. But what I've learned over the years is learning to accept each other's faults and choosing to celebrate each other's differences is one of the most important keys to creating a healthy, growing, and lasting relationship.

The person who submitted this story is anonymous.

"I CHOOSE"

I choose to live by choice, not by chance,
To be motivated, not manipulated,
To be useful, not used,
To make changes, not excuses,
To excel, not compete.
I choose great character, not bad character,
I choose to listen to my inner voice,
not to the random opinions of others.
I choose to do the things that others won't so I can
continue to do the things they can't.
Because, if I continue doing what I have been doing,
I will keep getting what I have been getting.
Therefore, I will act for best of my personal interest.

Author: Unknown

Here is a story I came across while I was reading on *positiveoutlooksblog.com* I decided to integrate it into this book so you could share it with your kid. They will take the message they need.

Paid In Full with One Glass of Milk

This is actually based on a TRUE EVENT.
Enjoy and be inspired!

Dr. Howard Kelly

One day, a poor boy who was selling goods from door to door to pay his way through school, found he had only one thin dime left, and he was hungry.

He decided he would ask for a meal at the next house. However, he lost his nerve when a lovely young woman opened the door. Instead of a meal he asked for a drink of water. She thought he looked hungry so brought him a large glass of milk. He drank it slowly, and then asked, "How much do I owe you?" "You don't owe me anything," she replied. "Mother has taught us never to accept pay for a kindness." He said… "Then I thank you from my heart."

As Howard Kelly left that house, he not only felt stronger physically, but his faith in God and man was strong also. He had been ready to give up and quit.

Years later, that young woman became critically ill. The local doctors were baffled. They finally sent her to the big city, where they called in specialists to study her rare disease. Dr. Howard Kelly was called in for the consultation! When he heard the name of the town she came from, a strange light filled his eyes. Immediately he rose and went down the hall of the hospital to her room.

Dressed in his doctor's gown he went in to see her. He recognized her at once. He went back to the consultation room determined to do his best to save her life. From that day he gave special attention to the case. After a long struggle, the battle was won.

Dr. Kelly requested the business office to pass the final bill to him for approval. He looked at it, and then wrote something on the edge and the bill was sent to her room. She feared to open it, for she was sure it would take the rest of her life to pay for it all.

Finally she looked, and something caught her attention on the side of the bill. She read these words… "Paid in full with one glass of milk" signed Dr. Howard Kelly. Tears of joy flooded her eyes as her happy heart prayed: "Thank You, God, that your love has spread abroad through human hearts and hands."

Dr. Howard Kelly (1895) was a doctor and founded the Johns Hopkins Division of Gynecologic Oncology at Johns Hopkins University.

Record your important thoughts and ideas on how to help your kid with **Building Character**

_____

_____

_____

_____

_____

_____

_____

_____

_____

_____

_____

_____

_____

_____

_____

_____

_____

_____

_____

_____

_____

_____

_____

Record your important thoughts and ideas on how to help your kid with **Building Character**

_____

_____

_____

_____

_____

_____

_____

_____

_____

_____

_____

_____

_____

_____

_____

_____

_____

_____

_____

_____

_____

_____

_____

_____

Record your important thoughts and ideas on how to help your kid with **Building Character**

_____

_____

_____

_____

_____

_____

_____

_____

_____

_____

_____

_____

_____

_____

_____

_____

_____

_____

_____

_____

_____

_____

_____

_____

_____

_____

_____

_____

Kids' Feelings

The question for this chapter is:
How do I make my kids feel good?

"Tough times never last, tough people always do."
~ Robert Herjavec,

A big part of positive parenting is helping your child to feel good about himself by nurturing his self-esteem without going overboard. It is important to realize that this does not come from catering to his every whim or showering him with insincere flattery, but by praising your child's legitimate accomplishments.

Keep in mind that these accomplishments can be as simple as dressing himself or feeding the dog without being asked, depending on your child's age and skill level. It also comes from using care when admonishing your child, and refraining from using demeaning or demoralizing words in your instruction. It is important to note that kids need to be allowed to do things on their own before you can praise them for the act, so don't be afraid to let your child experience age-appropriate independence as often as possible.

Another part of positive parenting includes catching your kids in the act of obedience, compassion or courtesy. It is amazing how many times every day a parent will say, **"No,"** or **"Don't,** instead of **"Yes,"** and **"Do."** What happens when you pass by your child's room, only to see him playing very nicely with his baby sister? Many parents will tiptoe past the scene so they do not disrupt the harmony that is playing out inside.

A better choice can be to stop and praise your child for showing kindness toward his sister and let him know how much you appreciate the fact that he takes his big brother responsibilities so seriously. This part of positive parenting can also encompass rewards for the obvious behaviors as well, such as a trip to the ice cream parlor for bringing home a stellar report card.

I added this quote as an extra bonus for this chapter. It was written by the great Mark Twain. It will help you and your kids avoid unwanted conversations that may end up hurting yours or his feelings.

"Never argue with stupid people, they will drag you down to their level and then beat you with experience."

~ Mark Twain

Be Positive: No surprise here; parents who express negative emotions toward their kids or handle them roughly are likely to find themselves with aggressive kindergartners. That's bad news, because behavioral aggression at different ages is linked to aggression later in life, even toward future romantic partners. So, if you find yourself in a cycle of the angry parent, angry baby, angrier parent, try to break free. It will ease your problems in the long run.

Last But Not Least, Know Your Kids. Everyone thinks they know the best way to raise a child. But it turns out that parenting is not one-size-fits-all. In fact, kids whose parents tailor their parenting style to the child's personality have half the anxiety and depression of their peers with more rigid parents, according to a study published in August 2011 in the *Journal of Abnormal Child Psychology*.

It turns out that some kids, especially those with trouble regulating their emotions, might need a little extra help from Mom or Dad. But parents can inadvertently hurt well-adjusted kids with too much hovering. The key, said lead researcher Liliana Lengua of the University of Washington is stepping in with support based on a child's cues.

Record your important thoughts and ideas on how to help your **kids feel good, better, & best!**

_____

_____

_____

_____

_____

_____

_____

_____

_____

_____

_____

_____

_____

_____

_____

_____

_____

_____

_____

_____

_____

_____

Record your important thoughts and ideas on how to help your **kids feel good, better, & best!**

_____
_____
_____
_____
_____
_____
_____
_____
_____
_____
_____
_____
_____
_____
_____
_____
_____
_____
_____
_____
_____
_____
_____
_____
_____

Record your important thoughts and ideas on how to help your **kids feel good, better, & best!**

_____

_____

_____

_____

_____

_____

_____

_____

_____

_____

_____

_____

_____

_____

_____

_____

_____

_____

_____

_____

_____

_____

_____

_____

_____

M☺tivati☺n

The question for this chapter is:
Will you motivate my kids in school?

Motivation is like bathing. It does not last forever. That is the main reason why Zig Ziglar recommends it every day.

Every time I deliver a motivational workshop to parents on how to raise positive kids in a negative world, parents ask me this question, "Do you go to schools to inspire and motivate kids?" The answer is, "Yes," parents recommend that I should go to every school possible. My response is, "Yes, I do motivate kids but it is the school that makes the final decision on whether or not I can come and motivate their students."

If you feel that it would be a great idea for me to come and motivate your kids in their school, go ahead and recommend my workshop to the decision maker of that school or private organization. Often it is the Community Liaison, Parent Coordinator, the Principal, or event coordinator who makes the decision.

I also speak in corporations, colleges, private organizations, churches, and every place where there are parents and/or entrepreneurs. Feel free to acquire a book as a gift for your loved one. They will be grateful to you for thinking of them.

What do I talk about when I motivate kids? I tell them my personal story. Once I have connected with them I tell them what they want to hear and blend with it what they need to hear. Overcoming adversity is a huge element in my talks because when kids are in school there are so many adversities for them to overcome that, if they are not inspired and/or motivated to go through the finish line, they will quit.

You do not want your kid to be a drop out. Neither do I. I want you to be able to be at peace knowing that your kid is getting the necessary motivation and information for his or her transformation.

Record your important thoughts and ideas about what it is that you learned overall from this great book. Share it with your friends.

Facebook.com/OVinspires

_____

_____

_____

_____

_____

_____

_____

_____

_____

_____

_____

_____

_____

_____

_____

_____

_____

_____

_____

_____

_____

_____

Record your important thoughts and ideas about what it is that you learned overall from this great book. Share it with your friends.

Facebook.com/OVinspires

_____

_____

_____

_____

_____

_____

_____

_____

_____

_____

_____

_____

_____

_____

_____

_____

_____

_____

_____

_____

_____

_____

_____

Record your important thoughts and ideas about what it is that you learned overall from this great book. Share it with your friends.

Facebook.com/OVinspires

_____

_____

_____

_____

_____

_____

_____

_____

_____

_____

_____

_____

_____

_____

_____

_____

_____

_____

_____

_____

_____

Made in the USA
Charleston, SC
06 March 2016